the
scars
that
made
me

Sarah White

Author's Note

This book is written under the pseudonym of Sarah White for privacy reasons. The poems are written from the perspective of a fictional speaker, created to express universal emotions and struggles. The author's goal is to provide a space for healing, reflection, and connection.

The purpose of this book is to offer solace to those who may have experienced similar pain, to remind them that they are not alone, and to provide a sense of comfort in facing the emotions often left unspoken. This collection is not just about the past; it is about finding the courage to heal, to forgive, and to embrace the possibility of a future where peace and love are not just distant dreams, but tangible realities.

Through this pseudonym, the author seeks to keep the focus on the story itself—on the journey through pain and toward healing. The goal is always to serve the readers who may find themselves reflected in these words, and to be a companion on their own path to healing.

to those who never knew
how it feels to be loved

contents

childhood scars

My mother taught me how to stand up straight,
how to clean the messes I didn't make,
how to keep my voice low
so no one would hear me cry.
She taught me that love
was something you earn,
not something you were given.

And I've spent my life
trying to unlearn it all.

The house I grew up in had rules.
Don't speak unless you're asked.
Don't cry unless it's for something real.
Don't ask for more than you're given.
I followed them all,
because the consequences
were heavier than the rules.
But no one told me
how to unlearn them.
Now, I'm an adult
still waiting for permission
to feel.

My mother's hands weren't kind.
They didn't hold mine,
didn't brush my hair,
didn't touch my shoulder
when I cried.
Her hands were always busy,
washing, scrubbing,
pointing to the things I did wrong.
I wanted them to rest,
to reach for me,
to hold me for no reason
other than because I was hers.
But they never did.

My mother never said, "I'm proud of you."
My mother never said, "You're enough."
Instead, she said,
"Don't embarrass me."
"Why can't you be like them?"
"Just do better."

Her words didn't leave scars,
but they made me small.
I started apologizing
for being myself,
for laughing too loud,
for asking too many questions,
for crying when I was hurt.
I carried her words with me
wherever I went,
waiting for someone, anyone
to tell me it's okay to be myself.

I became the quiet one,
the nice one,
the one who didn't need anything.
I learned how to smile
when I wanted to cry,
how to stay invisible
when the room was too loud.

I told myself it was better this way,
better to be small,
better to disappear
than to ask for too much.

But now, I wonder:
If I had let myself be seen,
if I hadn't tried so hard to be perfect,
would my mother have noticed me?

I didn't need my mom to have all the answers.
I didn't need her to fix everything for me.
I just wanted her to notice me,
to sit with me when things were hard,
to tell me it was okay
when my world was falling apart.
But she was always too busy
fixing everything else,
holding up the world
like it was her job.
And maybe it was.
But I still wish
she had saved some strength
for me.

I don't remember my mother saying "I love you."
Not in words,
not in the way I needed to hear it.
Her love was in folded laundry,
in packed lunches,
in rules that made me feel more trapped
than safe.
I know she tried her best,
but her best didn't feel like enough
when all I wanted
was to hear those 3 words.

I didn't need much.
Just someone to ask,
"Are you okay?"
and actually listen.
Instead, I learned to smile
even when everything inside me
was breaking.
I figured out how to pretend I was fine,
because no one ever stopped
to check on me.
And now,
I don't know how to say,
"I need help,"
without feeling like a burden.

Dad, you said you loved me,
but love isn't just words.
It's showing up,
staying when it's hard,
choosing me over the things
you were running from.
I needed you to show me
that love could be safe,
but instead,
you taught me how to fear it.

I loved my mother,
even when it hurt.
Even when her anger
left bruises on my heart
that no one else could see.
I stayed,
because daughters are supposed to stay.
But sometimes,
I wonder what it would feel like
to stop being her daughter
and just be me.

My mother gave me her strength,
but she gave me her pain too.
Her anger became mine,
her fear followed me everywhere.
She said she loved me,
but her love felt heavy,
something I had to carry,
not something that carried me.
I've tried to forgive her,
but forgiveness feels like letting her win,
like saying all the hurt she caused
was somehow okay.

Dear dad,

You were supposed to check for monsters
under the bed,
but instead, you became the reason
I stayed awake.

You were supposed to clap
when I showed you my drawings,
but you taught me to stop sharing
things I was proud of.

You were supposed to hold me
when the world felt heavy,
but your arms were the first weight
I ever learned to carry.

You were supposed to be my safe place,
but you taught me
that even home can hurt.

I didn't need a perfect dad.
I just needed one who stayed,
one who asked how I was
and actually listened.
I wanted to see pride in your eyes
when I did something good,
but I never did.
I wanted to hear your voice say,
"I'm here for you,"
but I never could.
Now, I don't even know
what it feels like
to be enough for you.

I learned early how to wear a mask,
a smile that made everyone
believe I was okay.
It keeps me safe, it hides the parts of me
I was too scared to show.

But now,
even when I want to take it off,
I don't know how.
The mask has been there so long,
it feels like part of my skin.

I'm afraid of what
people might see
if I let it slip,
the cracks, the tears,
the pieces of me
I don't know how to explain.

So I keep smiling,
because it's all I know how to do.
Even when it hurts,
even when I'm breaking,
I'm afraid that if I take it off,
no one will want to stay and
see the real me.

I learned that love
was something I had to earn.
I thought if I stayed quiet,
if I tried harder,
I'd finally be enough.
Now, I love like I'm always falling short,
like I have to give more
than I have,
just to keep it.
Even when someone says,
"I love you,"
I can't believe them.
I keep waiting to find out
what they want from me.

They say kids are supposed to laugh
to feel safe,
to know they're loved.
But I learned to stay quiet,
to keep my feelings to myself,
because no one ever asked
if I was okay.
I learned that hugs weren't for me,
that love was something other kids got,
that I wasn't someone
worth comforting.
Now they tell me
to let it go,
to move on,
to stop holding onto the past.
But how do I forget
what it felt like
to be overlooked?
How do I heal
when I never learned
what love is supposed to feel like?

Fathers don't always leave.
Sometimes they stay,
but their love doesn't.
They sit in the same room
but don't notice
the way you shrink yourself
to fit into their expectations.
They see your mistakes
but not your effort,
your tears
but not your reasons.
And you spend your whole life
trying to be enough
for someone
who doesn't see you at all.

My father left, but I still felt him everywhere.
I held his name like a promise,
like if I said it enough, he might come back.
I used to think if I was good enough,
quiet enough, easy enough,
he would find a reason to stay,
but I was wrong.
Some people don't leave because of you.
They leave because that's
all they know how to do.

My mother needed me more than I needed her,
but I didn't understand that then.
I thought if I held her tightly enough,
if I smiled through the weight of her grief,
it would be enough to fix her.
But love doesn't fix brokenness.
It just makes the weight harder to bear.

I remember waiting for
a father who never came.
I remember wondering if it was me,
If I was too much, or not enough.
I don't know if you ever think about me,
but I think about you.
But I've learned that people like you
don't come back, and people like me
learn to live with that.

My friends think I'm happy,
and I let them believe it.
It's easier than explaining
what I don't fully understand myself.
I learned how to smile
when everything felt like breaking.
I learned how to talk about nothing,
so they wouldn't ask about everything.

When they say I'm strong,
I don't correct them.
Because I'm afraid
that if they see the cracks,
they'd leave me.
So I stay quiet,
let them think I'm strong.
It's easier to lie
than to let anyone see the truth.

I gave them the love
I wished someone had given me,
the kind of love
that never asked for anything in return.
I stayed up late,
even when my own heart ached from exhaustion.
I put them first,
even when I couldn't remember
the last time someone asked if I was okay.
I let them lean on me,
when I was falling apart inside.
I listened to their pain,
while mine went unheard.
I did my best to be everything
I needed when I was younger,
but no one told me
how much it would hurt
to always give
and never receive.
I didn't realize
how empty I'd feel
after filling everyone else's cup
while mine stayed dry.

I became a second mother
without ever being asked.

I cleaned the mess,
answered the questions,
and carried the blame
for things I couldn't control.
When my siblings make mistakes,
it's my fault.
When my parents fight,
it's my job to be the mediator.

They call me strong,
but it doesn't feel like strength.
It feels like I was given a role
I never asked for.

My mother taught me that love hurts,
that I should stay quiet when I'm in pain,
that I should love people who hurt me.

My father taught me how to live without love,
how to stop expecting people to stay,
how to pretend it doesn't hurt when they walk away.

I wish they had taught me something else.
Because now, I don't know the difference
between love and pain.

Mom, you were supposed to be my first home,
but you became my first heartbreak.

I reached for your love
and found anger instead.
I wanted your warmth,
but your coldness was all I got.

You taught me how to crave
what I could never have.
You showed me how to love
people who hurt me
and call it loyalty.

And now,
every time someone leaves,
I wonder if it's my fault.
Because you taught me love
is something I have to earn,
not something that I was given.

Dear mom,

I thought mothers were supposed to heal,
but all you did was cause pain.

You gave me life,
but then you left me to figure out
how to live it alone.
I tried to love you,
but you made it feel impossible.

You taught me how to smile
when I felt invisible,
how to stay quiet
when everything inside me was screaming.

I wish you had taught me
how to feel loved
instead of teaching me
how to live without it.

As a child, I learned how to be quiet,
how to shrink myself into the background,
how to exist without being seen.
I learned that love has rules,
that some people only stay
when they can use you.
I learned how to smile when I was hurting,
how to say, '*I'm fine*' and
make it sound believable,
But the truth is, I never wanted much,
just to feel like I was enough..

While other kids laughed and ran,
I sat alone,
wondering what it felt like
to be included.

While other kids wished for magic,
I wished for someone to notice me,
to see past the smiles I faked
and ask me if I was okay.

I didn't want much.
Just a hand to hold,
just a voice that didn't hurt.
But as a child,
I learned how to make
loneliness my home.

As a child, I was taught
that emotions were weapons,
not something to be shared.
When I showed anger,
it became a fight.
When I showed sadness,
it was dismissed.
So, I learned to bury my feelings,
to keep them hidden
where no one could use them against me.
Now, I don't know how to let them out.
I don't know how to cry
without feeling like I've failed,
or how to speak my truth
without fearing it will be turned into a fight.
The silence feels safer,
but it's also the loneliest place to be.

I learned to swallow my pain,
because speaking up
only made things worse.

I taught myself to stay quiet,
to hold it all inside,
to disappear
so I wouldn't cause problems.

Now, I keep everything inside
until it spills out all at once,
and I'm left drowning
in everything I tried to hide.

I watched my mother
give everything she had
to a man who gave her nothing.

She called it love.
She called it sacrifice.
But all I saw
was her breaking.

Now, I catch myself
mistaking silence for peace,
and anger for love,
because no one ever taught me
what love was supposed to feel like

They say there's a difference
between being a good father
and being a good man.
A good father shows up,
but a good man knows how to f.
A good father provides,
but a good man listens.
A good father can teach you how to survive,
but a good man shows you how to feel safe.
My father was there,
but he was never present.
He gave what he thought I needed,
but never what I asked for.
And now, I wonder
if he ever saw the difference,
or if I was just another thing
he tried to fix
without ever asking
what was broken.

I wanted my father to be the kind of man
I could be proud of.
I wanted him to be the kind of man
I could look for in someone else.
Instead, I look for men
who remind me of him,
who make me feel the same ache
of being undesired.
I wanted him to show me
how to love without fear,
but all he taught me
was to never trust love.

You gave me your last name,
but not your time.
You gave me life,
but not your love.

You didn't teach me how to feel safe,
only how to keep quiet.
You didn't show me how to dream,
only how to stay mediocre.

I wanted to hear you say you were proud,
to see you look at me
like I mattered to you.
But all I ever saw
was your back as you walked away,
and all I ever felt
was that I wasn't enough for you.

My first heartbreak
wasn't from a boy.
It was from you, dad.

I thought fathers are supposed to
teach daughters what love should feel like,
but all you taught me
was what to avoid,
and I still got it wrong.

I have a father, but I never had a dad.
He was there, but I never felt his presence.
I think he tried to love me, but I could never feel it,
and maybe that's why I don't know what it feels like
to be loved by a man.

My father was my first heartbreak,
the first love I gave that was never returned.
I spent years hoping he'd see me,
but I was invisible in his eyes.
It took me too long to realize
that I could never make him love me,
no matter how hard I tried.

If real love means begging to be chosen,
then I want no part of it.
I'd choose loneliness every time.

I thought growing up
would mean leaving the past behind,
but I still feel like her,
the little girl who stayed quiet,
who didn't ask for anything
because she knew the answer would be no.
I still carry her fears,
her loneliness,
her need to prove
she's worth loving.
And no matter how much I grow,
she's always there,
waiting for someone to tell her
she's enough.

They say what doesn't kill you
makes you stronger,
but it only left me scared.
Scared of getting close,
because people always seem to take more than they give.
Scared of trusting,
because trust always ends in broken pieces.
Scared of loving,
because love has always felt
like a gamble I'm destined to lose.
Trauma didn't make me brave;
it made me afraid to try,
because trying has always felt
like the first step toward breaking.

One time after school when I was little,
I sat on the school steps by the car park
watching the cars disappear,
one by one.
The teacher asked if someone was coming.
I nodded, pretending I knew.

But I didn't.
I didn't know if anyone remembered me.

The air grew colder,
the sky turned dark,
and still, I waited.
Too scared to cry,
too ashamed to ask for help.

When my mom finally arrived,
there was no apology,
just a "you should've called."

That's the day I learned
it was my job
to make sure
I wasn't forgotten.

They say every child deserves a parent,
but I wonder if I ever deserved you.
You told me once,
the world was too much for you to carry
but wasn't I supposed to help you carry it?
Instead, you put me down like a burden
and walked away without looking back.
I waited for you,
for the words that never came,
for the love you never gave.
But waiting became like grieving,
and grieving became the only thing
I ever got from you.

I promised myself
I wouldn't become like my mom.
But some days,
her voice rises in my throat,
sharp and unforgiving.
I hear her in the way I say "no,"
in the way I slam doors
just to make a point.
Her anger feels like a language
I was born knowing,
and I wonder if I'll ever unlearn it.

I promised myself I'd be better,
but how do you stop yourself
from becoming the only version of love
you were ever shown?

My parents taught me how to stay quiet,
how to hide my tears
behind closed doors.
They taught me that love
wasn't something you felt,
it was something you endured.
I grew up believing
that pain was a part of love,
until one day,
I couldn't tell the difference
between the two.

I didn't ask to be the third parent,
to grow up before I was ready,
to learn how to calm storms
I didn't create,
or to give more than I ever got.

I was the one who stayed up late
wiping tears that weren't my own,
the one who cleaned up messes I didn't make.
I was the one that carried the blame
that was never mine to hold.

My siblings got to make mistakes
and take their time figuring things out.
I had to grow up fast
and be the one they looked up to,
even when I was breaking inside.

I became the "strong one"
before I even knew what strength was.
I didn't choose this role,
it chose me.

I'm the one who stayed up late
watching over everyone,
but no one ever stayed up for me.
I'm the one who said,
"It's okay, I'll take care of it,"
when what I really wanted to say was,
"can someone take care of me for once?"
I was the one who suffered the consequences of
my siblings' mistakes.

I didn't grow up, I raised myself.
I carried burdens too heavy for my shoulders,
hid my tears so no one else would break,
and learned too soon
that being strong meant being alone.

2

relationship scars

I told myself you loved me
every time you kissed my forehead,
every time you whispered "stay"
after tearing me apart.
You made the chaos feel like passion,
and I thought leaving
meant giving up on love.

You made me believe
love meant giving up parts of myself
so you could feel whole.
You fed me just enough hope
to make me forget
you were starving me.

"You're overreacting,"
was his favorite line.
As if my pain
was just another inconvenience
he didn't want to deal with.

When love
feels like walking on eggshells,
you learn to tiptoe so softly,
you forget how to stand.

I kept watering a dead plant,
thinking if I just tried harder,
it would come back to life.
I gave it everything,
time, patience, love.
I stayed up at night
asking myself what I was doing wrong,
why nothing I did was ever enough.
but no matter what I gave,
the leaves stayed brown,
the roots stayed dry,
and it never grew.
you were the dead plant.
and I was the fool
pouring my heart into something
that was never going to love me back.

When he says he's sorry,
remind him of the scars,
not the ones on your skin,
but the ones he left on your mind and heart.
Tell him about the countless hours you spent
staring at the ceiling hopelessly,
asking yourself
if you were too much or not enough,
when the truth is,
he never deserved you at all.

I wish I could show you my heart,
open it wide and let you see
the pieces you shattered.

If only you could see
the nights I spent staring at the ceiling,
unable to sleep,
the silence pressing on my chest
until it feels like I can't breathe.
I sit in the dark,
trying to piece myself together,
wondering why loving you
always felt like breaking.

Maybe then you'd know
what it's like to give everything
and still end up feeling
like nothing.

I don't regret knowing you.
I just regret the way
I let you build a home
inside me,
only to tear it down.

I don't regret knowing you.
I just regret the parts of myself
I gave away
just to keep you.

I don't regret knowing you.
I just regret the nights
I spent convincing myself
your love was enough,
even when it felt like nothing.
I don't regret knowing you.
but I can't help
wishing I had learned
to leave sooner.

I don't want to be her again,
the girl who pretended everything was fine,
who swallowed her pain
because she thought love meant sacrifice.

She believed your soft words,
even when your actions hurt.
She thought if she stayed,
you'd change,
but all it did was leave her empty
She let you in,
trusted you with her heart,
and now I'm left
picking up the pieces,
locking every door
she left open.

I don't want to be her again,
the girl who confused love with pain.

When people ask why we ended,
I don't know how to tell them
that love was like a rope
we kept pulling from both sides,
until I let go
because it hurt too much to hold on.
I don't know how to explain
that we were two puzzle pieces
that looked like they fit,
but left gaps no matter how hard we tried.

I don't know how to say
that staying felt like walking on thin ice,
but leaving felt like falling through it anyway.
So I just say,
"Sometimes love isn't enough."

He never asked how my day was.
He only noticed when my stomach wasn't flat,
when my breasts didn't sit high,
when my body didn't look like it did when we met.
His eyes always saw what had changed,
like I wasn't enough if I wasn't perfect.
It didn't matter who I was,
as long as I looked the way he wanted.

When I told him I felt invisible,
he laughed and said,
"How could anyone not see you?"
like my worth was only in my looks,
and that's all anyone would ever notice.

I'm not scared to love again,
I'm scared of giving my heart to someone
who doesn't see how fragile it is,
who will take it and break it
without even noticing.

I'm afraid of trusting someone
who won't see how hard it is
to love when you're already broken.

I never cared about being alone,
I was alone my whole life.
No one ever stayed long enough
to notice when I disappeared.
I got used to being in a room
full of people, but never really seen.
Being alone became my comfort.
It became a place where nothing could hurt me
because nothing was ever close enough.
I didn't need anyone,
I didn't have to explain myself.
I kept my walls high,
and no one ever had to know
what was really going on inside.

It was easier that way.
No one could disappoint me
if I didn't let them in.
I never felt empty that I was alone,
until you asked me to stay.

I stopped answering your calls,
not because I didn't care,
but because every time I did,
I felt like I was drowning.
You only reached out when it was convenient for you,
but never when I needed you most.
I became tired of always being the one to give,
while you took and never gave back.
I couldn't keep giving pieces of myself anymore
when you never noticed how much I was losing.

I walk on eggshells,
careful not to ask for too much,
and say sorry when I did nothing wrong.
When he pulls away,
I hold on tighter, trying to prove
I'm worth staying for.
I tell myself this is just how love is,
that pain is part of love,

He reminds me of my dad a lot.

The hardest part of our breakup
wasn't losing you,
but losing me.
I don't know who I am anymore.
I don't remember how to love myself
without you in the picture.
I still look for your approval
in everything I do,
like it's the only way I know how to exist.

You made me apologize,
while you were the one causing the pain.
I learned to say sorry for everything,
even when I had done nothing wrong.
You made me believe I was the problem,
that I wasn't enough,
and I kept trying to fix something
when I was never the one broken.
I gave you everything,
hoping you'd finally see me,
but you never did.

I keep saying I'll get out of bed today,
but I don't know how to face another day
without you.
I thought I could move on,
but everything feels empty without you here.
I tell myself I'll be fine,
but each day feels heavier than the last.
I wait for something to change,
for someone to pull me out of this hole,
but nothing ever happens.

I tried to fix what you broke,
but every time I put myself back together,
I found more pieces missing.
Was it you who broke me,
or was it me for believing
I wasn't enough without you?
I waited for your love to fill the gaps,
but all it did was leave me emptier.
I gave everything,
but you never gave anything back.

I think I broke myself.

He leaves you broken,
and you fix yourself just to break again.
You tell yourself you'll walk away,
but instead,
you run in circles,
searching for the love you never got

I was so naive,
I gave you everything I had,
and you never even noticed.
I thought you'd love me back,
but you never showed it.
Now I'm trapped loving someone
who never felt the same,
and I don't know how to walk away.

You were the answer to all my questions,
but the clock was ticking too fast.
I found you when I wasn't ready,
when everything in my life was falling apart.
I wanted to love you, I really did,
but I didn't know how to love myself first.
I wanted to give you all of me,
but I was still searching for who I was.
You gave me everything,
and I couldn't give you the same.
You felt like home,
but I wasn't ready to let you in.

I hope one day you realize
how much I truly loved you.
How I kept showing up
when you barely cared enough to stay.
I sacrificed my time and energy
just to make sure you never felt alone,
but in the end, it was only me
who was left empty.

I kept waiting for you to choose me,
but you only chose yourself.
And now, I'm left with nothing but broken pieces
of love I should've never had to fight for.

I loved you when you didn't care,
thinking maybe my love would change you.
But every day,
you showed me that love wasn't enough.
When you walked away,
I wasn't just losing you,
I was losing everything I thought
I knew about love.
Now I'm left wondering if I'll ever
be enough for anyone
after giving everything to someone
who never saw me.

I handed you my heart,
my most precious possession,
but you treated it like it was disposable.
You never wanted to hold it,
just to break it and walk away.
You took my love and shattered it,
like glass falling from a height,
watching it scatter across the floor
while I tried to pick up the pieces
of something I'll never put back together.

Stop wasting your energy
on people who don't care about you.
If they really cared,
they would've stayed,
but they didn't.

And it's not your fault.
You gave your heart,
but they took it for granted,
never realizing how precious it was.
You were never the problem,
but they made you feel like you were.
So don't keep blaming yourself.

You deserve someone who stays
not just when it's convenient,
but someone who chooses you.
Every. Single. Day.

I keep falling for people who remind me
of the love that broke me,
because it's all I ever knew.
I try to move on,
but I keep seeing fragments of the past
in the way they speak,
in the way they look at me,
in the way they leave when things get hard.
I can't help but hope
they'll give me the love I never got.
But maybe that's the only love my father ever taught me,
the kind that leaves me broken.

I became everything he needed,
and nothing I wanted to be.
I lost myself trying to fix him,
thinking it would make him love me more.
I gave pieces of myself I couldn't afford to lose,
hoping he'd notice,
but he never did.

Now, when I look in the mirror,
I barely recognize who I've become.
I changed myself into someone worse,
all for love I never got back.
I became what he wanted,
and forgot who I was along the way.

I stayed because I thought love was supposed to hurt,
that it was just part of the deal.
That's how my mother loved my father,
giving everything, even when it broke her.
I thought if I loved hard enough,
you'd love me back the way I needed.
But every day, I gave more of myself,
and you gave less.
I stayed because I didn't know any other way.
I thought pain meant I was doing it right,
but all it did was leave me broken.

You played with my heart like it was a game,
You'd give me just enough to keep me hooked,
then disappear when I needed you most.
You told me you loved me,
but your actions never matched your words.
And when I questioned you,
you twisted my words,
made me feel like I was the crazy one.
You gaslighted me into believing I was the problem,
when all along, you were the one breaking me.
I hate you for the pain you've caused,
but I hate myself more for staying so long,
for believing I could fix something that
was never mine to fix.

I have a habit of loving people
who don't know how to love me back.
I give them my heart,
but they hold it like it's a burden.
I stay, hoping they'll change,
hoping my love will be enough
to make them realize they're not alone.
But the truth is,
I'm the only one who's holding on,
while they keep slipping away.

I gave you my heart without hesitation,
but you never gave me yours.
I thought if I loved you enough,
you'd feel the same.
But every time I reached out,
you pulled away.
You loved me when it was convenient,
but never when I needed it the most.
I kept hoping you'd change.
I kept hoping that one day you'd realize
that my love wasn't something to be taken for granted.
But you never saw it,
and now I'm left with the weight of loving someone
who never understood how much I loved him.

I gave you everything I had,
but all you ever saw was what I didn't give.
I loved you in ways you never understood,
while you were never there each time I needed you close.
You told me I was too much,
but never that I was enough.
I gave you special pieces of myself,
thinking they'd bring us closer
but all they did was leave me empty.
I kept waiting for you to see me,
but you only saw what you wanted me to be.
I'm tired of holding on to this love.
And I don't know how to let go
of someone who never even tried to hold me.

You never loved me,
you only loved the version of me that existed
to please you.
I lost myself trying to be what you wanted,
hoping you'd see me,
hoping you'd care about what I needed.
But you never did.
You wanted someone who gave everything,
without asking for anything back.
I kept offering you all I had,
and you took it,
never realizing how much I was losing.

All you gave me was empty promises,
and the pain of loving someone
who never loved back.

3

mending the scars
(relationships)

I can't keep pretending that everything's fine,
but I can't keep holding on to something that's already gone.
I can't keep waiting for a love that isn't coming back.
But I do know this,
I'm letting go.

I'm done trying to hold onto something that's already broken.
I'm done fighting for someone
that doesn't want to fight for me.
I'm done with the anger, the hurt
the emptiness that trapped me for so long.
I've finally realized
that if I want peace,
I need to stop trying to fix what isn't mine to fix.

So this is me letting go,
and this time,
I'm not looking back.

Healing doesn't always look pretty.
Some days, you'll feel like the harder you fight,
the deeper you sink into the weight of everything
you thought you were leaving behind.

You'll stare at the pieces of yourself
that you're still trying to put together,
and wonder if you'll ever feel whole again.
But that's the thing about healing,
you don't realize how much you've grown
until you're standing on the other side,
and the pieces that felt like a burden
start to make sense.

Some days, it will feel like you're drowning,
like the pain is all there is.
But the truth is, you're only floating
waiting for the storm to pass.

Healing doesn't always look pretty,
but little by little, you'll find yourself again,
and one day, you'll know just how
strong you've become.

Every time I let you back in,
it felt like picking up a knife and
pretending it wouldn't cut me.
You never came back to stay.
You came back to make sure
you still had a way in,
that I was still willing to hurt for you.

So I put the knife down.
I stopped bleeding for someone
who only came to watch me suffer.
I let the wounds close, and
let the scars remind me that
some pain is meant to make you stronger
and teach you to never to go back.

I saw your text,
the text that said if we can just "talk,"
but I knew it wasn't really about talking.
It was about you wanting me to stay
in the same cycle we've been in,
asking me to relive the pain
because you didn't know how to let go.
You never asked if I was okay,
or how I was doing,
just if I was still willing to be there
when it suited you.

But this time I'm done.
I don't need to hold onto the past
just to prove I loved you.
I've learned that I am worth more
than the scraps you offer.

I'm choosing myself now,
I won't keep chasing someone
who was never really there.
It's time to give myself the love
you never could.

I thought finding myself again
would feel like coming home,
but it feels more like starting over,
like learning how to walk again.

I'm learning to forgive my self
for the years I spent lost,
and to take back the parts of me
I gave away just to feel loved.

And for the first time in a long time,
I'm not looking for someone else
to tell me who I am.
I'm deciding that for myself.

I didn't wait for someone to save me.
I saved myself,
When the world turned its back on me.
I picked myself up over and over,
and kept going, even when the weight of everything
felt like too much,
even when I felt broken beyond repair.
I learned to trust myself,
to believe that I was enough,
not because anyone told me,
but because I decided to not let my past
define me.
My strength isn't measured by what others see,
But by how far I've come alone.

We were never meant to last forever,
and maybe that was the lesson.
You taught me that love doesn't always stay,
and that's part of growing.
I'll remember what we had
without holding on to the things that weighed us down.
The lessons we learned,
the laughter, the tears, the fights,
all of it shaped who I am today.

But I won't keep holding on to what's in the past.
I won't let it control my future.
And one day, when I think of you,
it'll be with peace, not pain.
I'll smile at the memories we had
and be thankful for the chapter,
but I won't let it control my story
that's still mine to live.

I want to believe in love again,
but it's hard when my heart still remembers
how it felt to be broken.

I've spent so long pretending it didn't matter,
telling myself that love was a luxury
I wasn't meant to have.
I tell myself I'm fine alone,
that loneliness feels safer
than risking another goodbye.
But sometimes, I catch myself hoping,
hoping for hands that don't let go,
for someone who sees how broken I am
and stays anyway.

I want to believe in love again,
to stop holding my heart so tightly,
to let it open, just a little,
and trust that this time,
it won't be broken.

I used to think that love meant sacrifice,
that I had to lose myself for us to work.
But I've learned the hard way
that love shouldn't come at the cost of who you are.

I tried so hard to make you see me,
to make you understand that I was there,
that I mattered, too.

But I gave so much,
and in the end,
You could never return the love.

I've learned that love isn't about losing yourself
to make someone else happy.
It's about finding balance,
about loving with all your heart,
but not at the expense of your own soul.
I've spent so long looking for validation from you,
but now I know
that the validation I needed was always inside me.

I kept telling myself I wasn't enough,
That I could have been better,
That I could have loved harder.
I stayed, letting you take everything from me,
Thinking if I just gave more,
You'd finally see my worth.

But now, I see it clearly,
I was never the problem.
You just didn't know how to love me.
And it took too me long to realize
that my love wasn't the issue.
It was the way you never knew how to give it back.

The hardest part was letting myself stay
When I knew I should've walked away.
For so long, I thought it was my fault,
but now, I know it wasn't me.
I'm learning to stop justifying your actions
And start giving the love I gave you back to myself.

I didn't forgive you for you,
I forgave you for me.
Because holding onto the hurt
meant living in the prison
you built for me.

But forgiving isn't forgetting.
I remember every word that cut,
every silence that screamed louder than anger.
I remember the nights
I held myself together
because you didn't.

I carry those memories,
not to keep the pain alive,
but to remind myself
of what I survived.
They don't make me bitter,
they make me stronger.
Because now I know
what love should never feel like.

I didn't want the world,
just someone who made me
feel like I belong in theirs.
I didn't want much,
just someone who chose me,
who didn't make me fight
for a place in their heart.

But instead, I received
one-word replies,
broken promises, and
false hope that you actually cared.

Now, I'm done waiting.
I'm walking away from the life
I kept building around you.
I'm learning to stand taller,
to live without looking back,
and to leave the fragments of us
in the past, where they belong.

Healing can feel like being in a maze.
You bump into the same walls and
take the same turns, thinking you're
going nowhere.
But really, each step, each turn,
is leading you closer to the exit.

Some days, you'll feel stuck,
like the walls are closing in,
and you'll question why you're even trying.
But every mistake, every step back,
is just another lesson,
another piece of the puzzle that's
falling into place.

It's okay to not have it all figured out,
to feel lost and confused.
You're finding your way,
even when it doesn't feel like it.
Each time you stand back up,
you're one step closer to freedom,
to the person you're meant to be.

So keep moving,
even when it feels like you're going nowhere.
Don't stop now, you're closer than you think.

I let go because love shouldn't feel like I'm drowning.
I gave you everything,
but you never noticed.
You never saw how much I was fading,
how much I was losing myself trying to hold on.

It wasn't your fault,
I let myself believe
that if I loved hard enough,
you'd love me back.
But I can't keep sacrificing myself
for a love that was never real.

Letting go was the hardest thing I've ever done.
It made me realize that love isn't worth it
if you don't love yourself first.

I used to think loneliness was a problem to fix,
like I wasn't enough on my own.
I spent years chasing after people,
hoping they would make me feel whole,
but I was only left feeling emptier.

Now I see that being alone doesn't mean
I'm missing something.
It's where I learned to love myself,
to be okay with just me.
I don't need anyone to make me feel complete anymore.
I'm finally learning that I was always enough.

This time, I'm not waiting for someone else to fill the space.
I'm filling it with my own love.

4

mending the scars
(childhood)

For so long,
I waited for an apology
from my parents
that would never come.
I told myself I needed it
to feel whole again,
to finally let go.

But I've learned
you can't heal by
waiting for someone else
to take responsibility.
Healing comes
when you stop hoping
they'll be sorry,
and start choosing yourself instead.

I don't hate my parents,
even though they gave me
all the pieces of their pain.

I just wish they had shown me
what to do with it,
how to hold it
without letting it bury me,
how to heal
without feeling guilty for it.

I grew up thinking love
meant carrying everything alone,
but I'm learning now
that I can set it down,
that I can forgive them
without losing myself.

Some wounds never fully heal,
but they don't define me.
I'm learning to live with them
and still find peace.

My father never asked for my forgiveness,
but I gave it to him anyway,
not because he deserved it,
but because I was tired of carrying
the heavy weight of his mistakes
and everything he left behind.

I still wish he had said sorry,
not just with words,
but with the way he looked at me,
like I was his daughter,
not one of his regrets.

I wanted him to see me, not just my flaws or failures,
but the child who waited for him every time he left,
long after he stopped coming back and showing up.

But now I know I don't need his apology
to let go of the pain he gave me,
or the anger I carried for so long.
I don't need his love to finally love myself.

I was born into a cycle of hurt,
a cycle of shame, fear, and neglect,
but I refuse to carry it any longer.
I choose a different path now,
one where love doesn't come with pain,
one where my worth isn't tied to what I give,
but to who I am.
I'll teach my children a different way,
a way of healing, not hurting.
I will break the cycle,
of generational pain.

I was raised by a mother who taught me
that my worth was measured by how much I could give.
I learned early that I only mattered
when I was needed, and that love
meant sacrificing yourself for others.
I spent years trying to prove I was worthy,
and gave everything I had to offer.

I'm learning to take back what I gave away,
to stop tying my worth to what I do for others.
Healing is about finding myself again,
loving the parts of me I once buried,
and realizing I'm enough, just as I am.
For the first time, I'm learning to love myself
without needing to give anything in return.

I spent years chasing approval
from parents, from lovers, from friends,
thinking if I could just be enough for them,
I'd finally be enough for myself.
But no matter how much I wanted to be validated,
I always felt unworthy inside.
It wasn't until I stopped looking for others to praise me
that I began to understand what true peace feels like.
I'm learning that loving myself
isn't about proving my worth,
but about accepting who I am.
The validation I've been searching for
was always inside me all along.

Forgiving you doesn't mean
I've forgotten, Mom.
I remember everything,
the words that hurt,
the broken promises,
the moments I needed comfort from you
but learned to be on my own instead.

I remember staying quiet,
not because I wanted to,
but because I thought it would
make you love me better.

Forgiveness isn't about erasing the pain;
it's about accepting that it happened
and choosing not to let it define me.
I forgive you, Mom,
but that doesn't mean the pain
you caused is gone.

I am my mother's daughter after all.
Maybe that's why I keep holding onto people
even when they hurt me.
I learned from her
how to hide behind a mask
even when everything inside me is breaking.

I see her in myself,
in the way I give at the cost of myself,
in the way I carry guilt
for things that were never my fault.
I see her in the pieces of me
I'm still trying to forgive.

But being her daughter
isn't just about the pain.
It's about learning to carry her love
without letting it break me,
to accept that she did her best,
even though it wasn't enough.

When I look into my mother's eyes,
I see the pain she carries,
the kind that begs for a second chance.
She wants to say sorry,
but the words get lost
somewhere between her heart and her mouth.

I wish I could go back in time,
to the little girl she once was.
I'd hug her tightly,
give her the love she never knew how to give,
and whisper,
"Don't let the ones who broke you
teach you what love is."

Maybe then,
she could have loved me
without the weight of her pain,
without the fear
that love would only break her again.

You existed in my life, but you were never really there.
In your neglect, I became the child who learned to
survive,
but never knew how to feel loved.
In your silence, I became a teenager who pretended
everything was fine,
even when I was falling apart inside.
The teenager who locked her heart away,
too scared it would break if she let anyone in.
In your absence, I became the young woman who
searched for love in all the wrong places,
because I didn't know how to give it to myself.
Without you, dad, I finally saw my worth and
loved myself,
because I learned I didn't need anyone to
make me feel whole but myself.

To my inner child,

I'm sorry you never knew what it felt like to be truly seen,
or to be held when the world felt too heavy.
I'm sorry you spent so much time waiting for a love
that was never there when you needed it most.
You were raised in a broken home,
with a mother who couldn't love you the way you deserved,
and a father who disappeared long before
you could understand why.

You gave love so freely,
but it was never returned.
You learned that love wasn't something you could ask for,
it was something you had to earn.
Maybe that's why you tried to fix everything,
hoping that if you made everything okay,
someone would finally love you back.
But no one ever did,
and that's not your fault.
You loved with everything you had,
even when no one loved you the same.
But now I know,
you were never meant to carry it all alone.
I'm sorry I wasn't there sooner
I'll never let you feel that way again.

My childhood trauma didn't make me stronger,
it made me believe that I could only be loved
by fixing everything around me.

I learned to be the quiet one,
the people pleaser,
hoping that if I was enough for everyone else,
someone would finally see me.
But no matter how hard I tried,
I was never enough for myself.
I thought if I could just give more,
if I could please enough people,
maybe I'd earn the love I was starving for.

I've spent my whole life thinking
that my worth was something I had to prove,
that love was something I had to work for,
even if it meant losing myself along the way.

But now, I see healing doesn't come from
what I gave up or offered.
It comes from embracing the hurt,
the pain I never let myself feel,
the fear that taught me to hide
the parts of me I thought were too broken to love.

I used to think I had to prove that
I was worthy of love,
but no one ever showed me
how to love the parts of me
I thought were too broken to heal.

Your parents couldn't love you the way you needed,
and it was never your fault.
They were broken too,
and couldn't give you the love
you needed.

It's okay to forgive them,
not because they deserve it,
but because you deserve the peace
that comes from letting go.
You've carried their neglect for too long,
and it has torn you apart.

Forgive yourself too for chasing
love in all the wrong places.
You didn't know any better.
You were just trying to fill a hole
in your heart that no one could fill
but you.

One day, you'll realize that happiness
was never found in someone else's arms,
It was always about learning to love
the pieces of yourself
you thought were too broken to keep.

I built a wall around my heart long ago
to keep the hurt out,
but the little girl inside me
was trapped in it,
hiding in the dark,
too scared to call for help.

As I grew, so did the wall,
higher, thicker,
a fortress I thought
would keep me safe.
Every brick was a moment
I felt unloved,
every stone was a broken promise.
But it wasn't protection;
it was her prison.
A constant reminder
that she was unworthy of love.

Now, I'm tearing it down,
brick by brick, stone by stone.
But she's still too afraid to come out,
unsure if freedom is worth
the risk of being hurt again.
I sit beside her, whispering softly,
"It's safe now, I promise.
I'll shield you from the hurt,
I'll hold you when it's too much.
You don't have to be brave alone anymore."

I thought a mother's love was supposed
to be unconditional,
but it always felt like something I had to earn.
I wasn't enough as I was,
I had to be quieter, more perfect,
just to get a little bit of affection.
I learned to seek approval before love,
and carried that need for validation
into every relationship I had.

Love should have been simple,
just something you feel, not something you have to prove.
But I've spent too long loving with strings attached,
wondering if I was ever enough.
Now I see that real love isn't about proving yourself,
it's about being loved for who you are,
even when you're broken, messy, and imperfect.

Mom, you told me I was too much,
too loud, too sensitive.
I spent years shrinking myself
to fit your idea of who I should be.
I made myself small,
hoping you would notice me,
hoping you would love me.
But no matter how much I gave,
how much I tried,
I was always too much or not enough.
You couldn't love me the way I needed,
and for so long,
I thought it was my fault.

I'm starting to see that
I am not your mistakes,
I am not your disappointments.
I don't need your love
to feel complete.
I have learned to love myself
without needing your approval.
I am enough, just as I am.

I've buried my pain deep inside me,
in places even I was afraid to look.
I thought it would stay there forever,
that I'd never feel whole again,
but I was wrong.

Healing isn't forgetting.
It's learning to live with the scars,
to see them not as flaws
but as proof
that I made it through.

I remember the nights
when it felt impossible to keep going,
when I thought I would never escape
the shadows of my past.
But somehow, I made it through,
and now, I'm finally learning to breathe again.

I've learned to love the parts of me
I once thought were broken.
I've learned to hold my own heart,
with kindness and care
I've learned to forgive myself
for believing I was ever unworthy.

No matter how much of my childhood was taken,
I refuse to let it define me.
I've turned my pain into lessons,
and my scars into strength

What was stolen from me is gone,
but what I build now is mine,
a life on my own terms,
free from the weight of my past.

Acknowledgement:

I would like to extend my deepest gratitude to everyone who has been a part of this journey.

First and foremost, to those who have experienced the deep pain and heartache that these poems speak to, I honor your strength and resilience. It is from your stories, your struggles, and your bravery that these words were born.

Finally, to the readers who pick up this book, who find pieces of their own story within these words: this is for you. Thank you for allowing these poems to connect with you, to be part of your healing. Your courage and openness mean the world.

This book is not just my journey—it's ours.

For the people who want to see more, you can find me on social media @sarahwhitepoetry or @thescarsthatmademe.

17063742R00075